MIND-BLOWING SCIENCE EXPERIMENTS

FANTASTIC EXPERIMENTS WITH

FORCES

Thomas Canavan

Gareth Stevens
PUBLISHING

Please visit our website, www.garethstevens.com.
For a free color catalog of all our high-quality books,
call toll free 1-800-542-2595 or fax 1-877-542-2596.

Cataloging-in-Publication Data

Names: Canavan, Thomas.
Title: Fantastic experiments with forces / Thomas Canavan.
Description: New York : Gareth Stevens Publishing, 2018. I Series: Mind-blowing science experiments I Includes index.
Identifiers: ISBN 9781538207499 (pbk.) I ISBN 9781538207437 (library bound) I ISBN 9781538207314 (6 pack)
Subjects: LCSH: Force and energy--Experiments--Juvenile literature. I Science--Experiments--Juvenile literature. I
    Science projects--Juvenile literature.
Classification: LCC QC73.4 C317 2018 I DDC 531.113--dc23

Published in 2018 by
Gareth Stevens Publishing
111 East 14th Street, Suite 349
New York, NY 10003

Copyright © Arcturus Holdings Limited

Author: Thomas Canavan
Illustrator: Adam Linley
Experiments Coordinator: Anna Middleton
Designer: Elaine Wilkinson
Designer series edition: Emma Randall
Editors: Joe Harris, Rebecca Clunes, Frances Evans

Photographs by Shutterstock.

Printed in China

CPSIA compliance information: Batch CS17GS: For further information contact
Gareth Stevens, New York, New York at 1-800-542-2595.

Having Fun and Being Safe

Inside this book you'll find a whole range of exciting science experiments that can be performed safely at home. Nearly all the equipment you need will be found around your own house. Anything that you don't have at home should be available at a local store.

We have given some recommendations alongside the instructions to let you know when adult help might be needed. However, the degree of adult supervision will vary, depending on the age of the reader and the experiment. We would recommend close adult supervision for any experiment involving cooking equipment, sharp implements, electrical equipment or batteries.

The author and publisher cannot take responsibility for any injury, damage or mess that might occur as a result of attempting the experiments in this book. Always tell an adult before you perform any experiments, and follow the instructions carefully.

Contents

A note about measurements

Measurements are given in U.S. form with metric in parentheses. The metric conversion is rounded to make it easier to measure.

Whether you're lifting books with your breath or examining moon-like craters in a baking tray, you'll be able to demonstrate how scientific forces are at work behind just about everything!

Some Light Reading

A pile of textbooks is pretty heavy to carry around, isn't it? But can you imagine lifting that same pile using just your breath? It seems easy enough to lift a sheet of paper or a feather with just your breath, but something as heavy as a stack of books? Is there a scientific trick waiting to be learned?

YOU WILL NEED

- 3 hardbound books (about 200 pages each)
- Masking tape
- Plastic drinking straw
- A small plastic bag
- Table

1

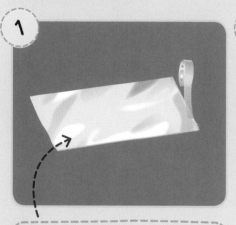

Tape the handle and open end of the bag shut, leaving just enough space to slide a straw inside it.

2

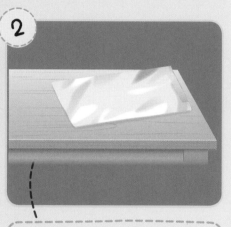

Place the bag close to the edge of the table, with the taped end facing you.

3

Pile the books on the bag.

4

Slide the straw into the gap in the bag and blow into it. The bag will begin to inflate and lift the books.

5

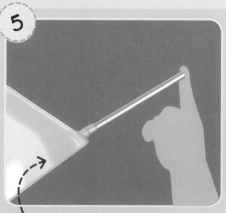

Stop to catch your breath, blocking the end of the straw to stop air from escaping.

6

Continue inflating the bag until the books have risen up about 1-2 inches (3-5 cm).

HOW DOES IT WORK?

You've just demonstrated Pascal's Law, first noted by French scientist Blaise Pascal in the seventeenth century. It deals with **fluids**, the term that scientists use to describe both **liquids** and **gases**. The law describes what happens if an outside **force** (in this case, your breath) is applied to an enclosed fluid (the air inside the bag). The force is transmitted equally throughout the fluid. You might think that your breath is a small force, but it is pressing equally all across the bag. That multiplied force then becomes strong enough to lift the books!

TOP TIP!

Make sure that the straw fits snugly inside the opening of the bag, with no gaps. You might even find it easier to slide the straw in first and then tape the end of the bag shut.

WHAT HAPPENS IF...?

Maybe you've done a variation of this experiment—in reverse. If you poke a blown-up balloon, you'll see it bulge out in all directions. That's because the force of your finger's **pressure** has been spread equally through the air inside the balloon. With enough force, it will burst!

REAL-LIFE SCIENCE

Have you ever seen a car lifted high up, so that a mechanic can work on its underside? It rises on a hydraulic jack. The jack that lifted the car worked on the same principle as your inflating bag—except that it was liquid (not air) receiving the extra force.

Last Man Standing

YOU WILL NEED

- 3 empty fruit juice cartons with screw-on caps
- Water
- Felt-tip pen
- Table
- Ruler
- Note pad

Here's a chance to scientifically define the term "pushover." Which of these three similar cartons is the easiest to knock down? You might be surprised at the result!

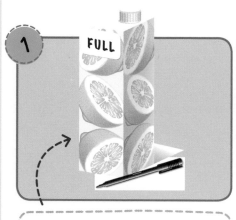

1 Fill one carton with water, screw the cap back on and mark it "Full."

2 Half-fill a second, replace the cap and mark it "Half."

3 Screw the cap back on to the third carton and mark it "Empty."

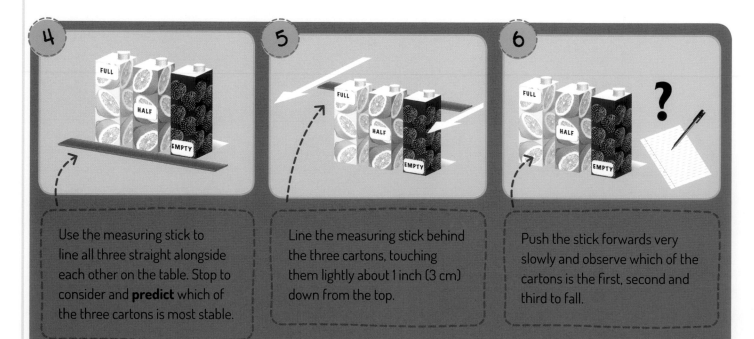

4 Use the measuring stick to line all three straight alongside each other on the table. Stop to consider and **predict** which of the three cartons is most stable.

5 Line the measuring stick behind the three cartons, touching them lightly about 1 inch (3 cm) down from the top.

6 Push the stick forwards very slowly and observe which of the cartons is the first, second and third to fall.

6

HOW DOES IT WORK?

This experiment is all about **center of mass**—the point in any object that represents the average location of its **mass**. You can imagine all of the object's mass being concentrated at that point. In practical terms, the center of mass determines how stable an object is. If it remains above the object's base of support (like the base of the cartons), then the object remains stable. The center of mass of the full—and empty—cartons was about halfway up the carton. But the half-full carton's center of mass was in the lower half because the top half (filled with air) had less mass.

TOP TIP!

Make sure that you have the measuring stick actually touching all three cartons before you move them.

WHAT HAPPENS IF...?

You could do this experiment over and over, filling the cartons to different levels, to find the amount of water that leads to the most stable result. Your first version showed that the carton with some water worked best. Would a one-third full carton be more secure? What about a carton that is ¼ full?

REAL-LIFE SCIENCE

The center of mass is important in all kinds of areas—from industry to entertainment. Just think of a group of acrobats forming a pyramid. If you drew an imaginary line down from the top acrobat's center of mass, it would end up safely in the middle of the person at the bottom (the base).

Up to the Water Mark

YOU WILL NEED

- 3 empty 2-liter plastic bottles
- Water
- Sharp pencil or nail
- Paper
- Ruler or tape measure
- 3 friends

We know that firefighters use hoses that work under enormous pressure to send the water great distances—high up into tall buildings, for example. But you don't need special equipment to understand how water behaves when it's under pressure.

1

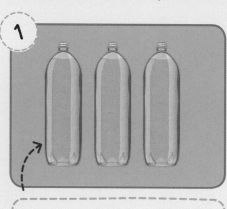

Fill each bottle completely with tap water.

2

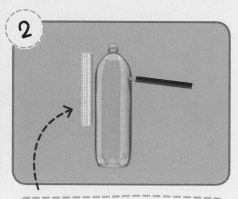

Ask an adult to make a hole as wide as the pencil in the first bottle, about 2 inches (5 cm) from the top. Ask a friend to plug the hole with their finger.

3

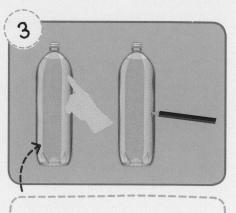

Repeat step 2 for the second bottle, but with the hole about halfway down.

4

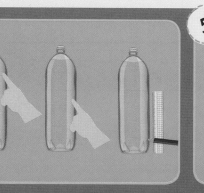

Repeat step 2 on the third bottle, poking the hole 1 inch (3 cm) from the bottom. Each friend should now be plugging a bottle.

5

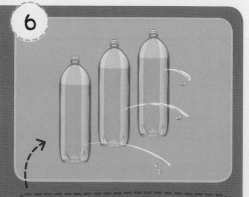

Line the bottles up about 2 feet (60 cm) apart, with the holes pointing in the same direction. Ask your friends to pull their fingers away from the bottles, one by one.

6

Watch how far each stream of water shoots and measure the distance. Which stream went the farthest?

HOW DOES IT WORK?

One of Sir Isaac Newton's great observations was that a force is a combination of something's mass and **acceleration**. In each water bottle, the water was falling with the same acceleration because of the force of **gravity**. The big difference between the three bottles was how much mass was bearing down on the water by each hole. The bottom hole had nearly a full bottle of water weighing down on it. All that extra mass meant more force, which is why this bottle shot its water the farthest!

TOP TIP!

Things can get a little messy, so make sure you do this experiment outside!

WHAT HAPPENS IF...?

You've worked out how the extra mass of water creates a stronger pressure, forcing the water out farther as the pressure increases. What if you did the experiment with larger or smaller holes in the bottles? Would the difference in "shooting length" remain the same?

REAL-LIFE SCIENCE

You've probably experienced the relationship between water pressure and depth when you've been swimming. The deeper you swim, the more pressure you feel, especially on your ears (which are sensitive to pressure). It's the same principle that explains the science behind this experiment.

The Attractive Balloon

YOU WILL NEED

- A party balloon
- At least six light plastic cups
- Some water

You want guests to stick around at your birthday party, but plastic cups sticking to a party balloon? That's not the right idea. How did those cups end up stuck to the balloon in the first place? A party game gone wrong? Time to investigate.

1

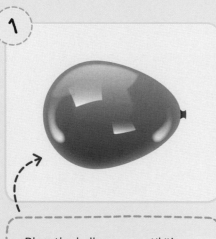

Blow the balloon up until it's about the size of a grapefruit.

2

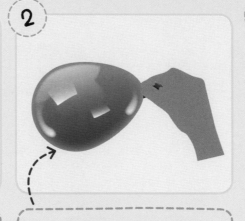

Pinch the balloon shut, but don't tie it.

3

Rub some water on the rims of six plastic cups.

4

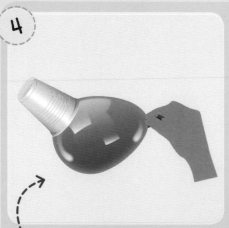

Press the rim of a cup tightly against the side of the balloon and then remove your hand. The cup should stay in place.

5

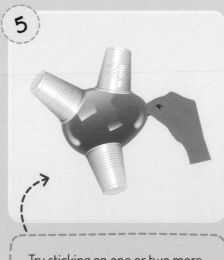

Try sticking on one or two more cups in the same way.

6

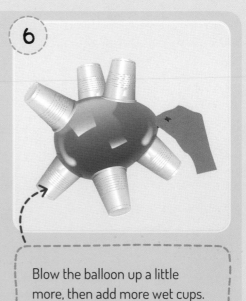

Blow the balloon up a little more, then add more wet cups.

10

HOW DOES IT WORK?

This experiment is an exploration of air pressure and **surface tension**. First, the wet surfaces of the rims helped the cups stick to the surface of the balloon. This is because of a force called surface tension. Each cup contained air. As you inflated the balloon more, the surface of the balloon flattened a little, so that the trapped air took up more **volume** (space) in the cup. This meant the trapped air lost some of its pressure. But the outside air pressure remained the same, forcing the cups against the balloon.

TOP TIP!

It's easier to do this experiment with a friend. They can add the cups while you blow the balloon.

WHAT HAPPENS IF...?

Lots of science experiments work if you "scale up" or "scale down." This means using larger or smaller amounts of ingredients to achieve the same result on a different scale. Can you imagine trying this experiment at the seaside, using a beach ball and some plastic buckets? Where else can you imagine performing a version of this experiment?

REAL-LIFE SCIENCE

Have you ever gotten your boots stuck in the mud? They might have even stayed locked in place when you tried to move! That's the power of air pressure. There was little or no air below your boots to press up, but the air pressure all around the boot still pressed down.

Falling Prices

A playing card, a coin, and an unexpected twist? Your friends might mistake this mind-blowing experiment for magic! Follow these steps to wow your audience with the wonders of **inertia**!

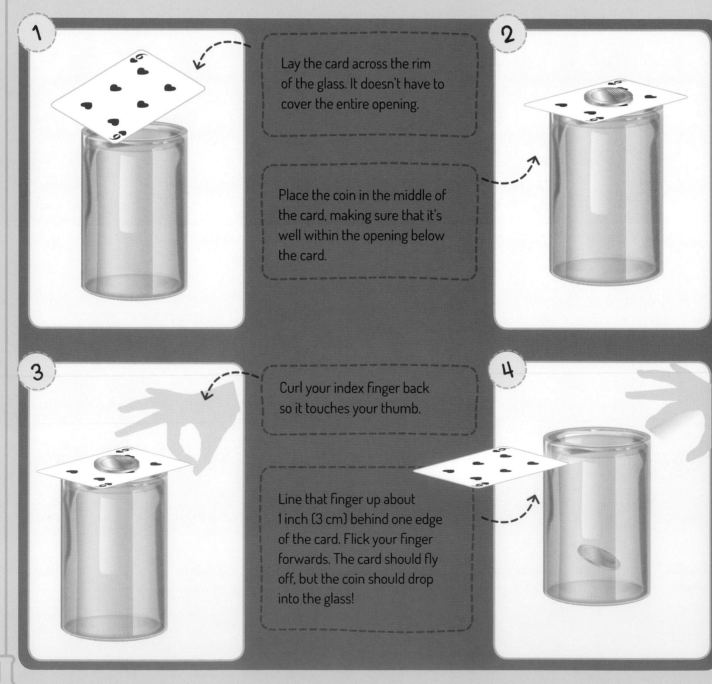

1. Lay the card across the rim of the glass. It doesn't have to cover the entire opening.

Place the coin in the middle of the card, making sure that it's well within the opening below the card.

2.

3. Curl your index finger back so it touches your thumb.

Line that finger up about 1 inch (3 cm) behind one edge of the card. Flick your finger forwards. The card should fly off, but the coin should drop into the glass!

4.

HOW DOES IT WORK?

This experiment is an excellent demonstration of Newton's First Law of Motion, which states that an object will stay at rest or will continue moving unless an outside force acts on it. That "unwillingness to move" (or the unwillingness to slow down if it's already moving) is called inertia, and it increases as something gets more mass. If you moved the card slowly, the force of that movement wouldn't overcome the force of the friction holding the coin in place. The much greater force of the flick overcomes the friction, so the object with less inertia (the less massive card) moves, but the coin doesn't.

TOP TIP!

This experiment works best with a clear glass. Hearing the "ping" when the coin falls in is extra satisfying!

WHAT HAPPENS IF...?

Can you imagine setting a table with crystal glasses and fine china, and then quickly whisking off the tablecloth from beneath everything? This classic magic trick uses the same principle as your experiment, and nothing breaks! But it takes a lot of practice to master this trick, so it's best to stick to coins and playing cards for now.

REAL-LIFE SCIENCE

You can see and feel the effects of Newton's First Law all the time. If you're in a car that stops suddenly, your body moves forwards. That's why we wear seat belts! If the same car moves forwards suddenly, you can feel yourself being pressed back into the seat. These are both examples of inertia.

Arch Power

You and your friends can build a medieval cathedral in your kitchen in a matter of minutes—or at least demonstrate one of the most important engineering features that has kept cathedrals standing for centuries. It's all about arches.

1

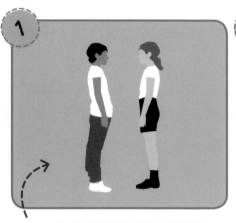

Have two of your friends stand facing each other, wearing just their socks.

2

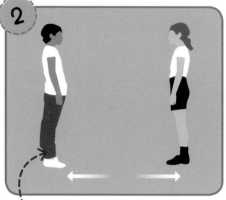

Ask them each to take one step backwards.

3

Ask your second pair of friends to sit on the floor behind the first pair. Your friends sitting down should wear shoes. The sitting friends' backs should touch the standing friends' calves.

4

Ask the first pair to keep their feet in place and to hold their arms up.

5

Have them lean forwards so that their hands meet. They are now forming an arch.

6

Ask the sitting pair to describe whether they can feel the force pushing out from the arch.

HOW DOES IT WORK?

The seated pair of friends should have felt the force of the others' heels digging into them. That's because the standing pair created an arch, and an arch is an important way of transferring forces. It takes the force of its own weight and any weight pressing on it (like the roof of a building) and transfers it into an outward and downward force along its curves. That's the force that the seated pair of friends can feel, pressing out from the heels of the two friends standing. Engineers call the supports at the base of arches (like the seated pair) buttresses.

TOP TIP!

This experiment works best if the sitting pair of friends keeps their shoes on to act as brakes against sliding (and to concentrate the force on their backs).

WHAT HAPPENS IF...?

With your four friends demonstrating how an arch works, you could work out how strong it is by measuring how much force it can transfer before breaking. Ask the standing pair to form fists before making an arch, then add book after book on to the level space along the back of their hands.

REAL-LIFE SCIENCE

Builders and engineers working nearly a thousand years ago used the principle of the arch as they built great cathedrals. At first, they built thick buttresses against the outside walls. Then they realized that even the buttresses could be arch-shaped to do their job. Those supports are called flying buttresses.

Low PresSure Affront

YOU WILL NEED

- Large kitchen mixing bowl
- Plastic bag (its mouth must fit over the bowl)
- Large rubber band
- 1 or more friends

How much does a plastic bag weigh? Could you pick one up? If you think this is a trick question—it is! You can use some simple science to "lock" a plastic bag inside a bowl. At least, that's how it will feel when you try to pick it up!

1

Open the bag and use it to line the inside of the bowl.

2

Press it snugly down and fold the spare plastic over the rim of the bowl.

3

Secure the outer plastic to the bowl with the rubber band.

4

Hold the bowl and ask a friend to pinch the middle of the bag and pull it out of the bowl. It should be very difficult, or impossible.

HOW DOES IT WORK?

You've just demonstrated Boyle's Law. This scientific principle is all about volume and pressure. It tells us that if the same amount of gas (measured in the amount of **molecules**) is forced into less volume, then its pressure increases. So, if the volume increases, the pressure goes down. That's what happens here when your friend pulls on the bag. Even a little tug increases the volume and lowers the air pressure inside the bag. But the air pressure all around you hasn't changed, and it wins the battle of the pressures, holding the bag down.

TOP TIP!

It doesn't matter whether you use a **ceramic** or metal bowl, as long as it's sturdy. You don't want the strength of the band to squeeze the bowl out of shape.

WHAT HAPPENS IF...?

So it's the outside air, which hasn't lost any pressure, that wins this battle. What do you suppose would happen if you used a much bigger bowl and bag? Or a smaller pair? Think about how scientists might measure the pressure exerted over a particular area, and you might find it easier to predict.

REAL-LIFE SCIENCE

You've probably seen someone blow up an empty plastic or paper bag, twist it shut, and slam down on it with their palm to burst it with a loud pop. That's another example of Boyle's Law. The air (a gas) inside got squeezed into a smaller volume and built up pressure—until it burst the bag open.

Crater Making

YOU WILL NEED

- Metal baking tray
- Hot cocoa mix or instant coffee
- Flour
- Spoon
- 3 playing marbles (of different sizes)
- Ruler

You've seen images of **craters** on the surface of the Moon and some planets, such as Mercury. Have you ever wondered what creates them, or why they're not all the same size? Time for some space exploration—in your kitchen!

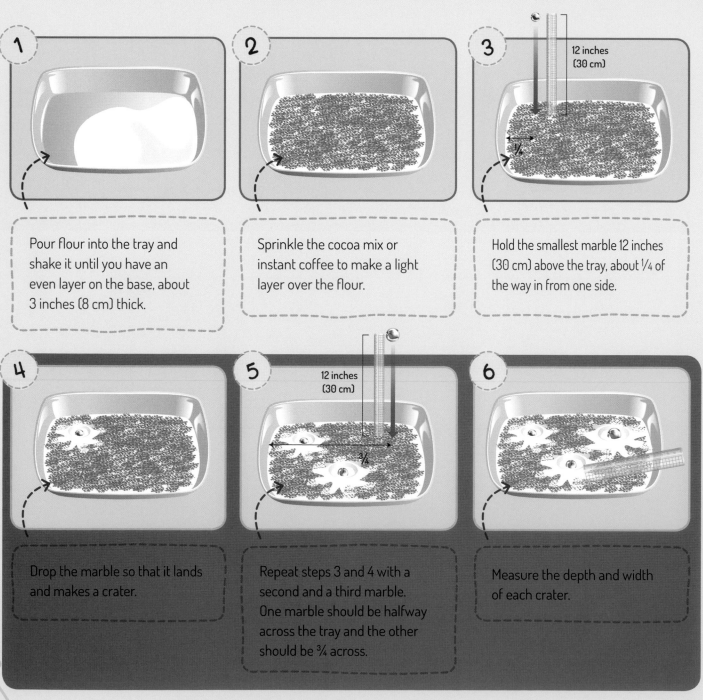

1 Pour flour into the tray and shake it until you have an even layer on the base, about 3 inches (8 cm) thick.

2 Sprinkle the cocoa mix or instant coffee to make a light layer over the flour.

3 Hold the smallest marble 12 inches (30 cm) above the tray, about ¼ of the way in from one side.

12 inches (30 cm)

4 Drop the marble so that it lands and makes a crater.

5 Repeat steps 3 and 4 with a second and a third marble. One marble should be halfway across the tray and the other should be ¾ across.

12 inches (30 cm)

6 Measure the depth and width of each crater.

HOW DOES IT WORK?

Newton's Second Law of Motion deals with force, the mass of an object, and its acceleration. Acceleration isn't always about speeding up—it can also be about slowing down. That's what these three marbles are doing. They're each slowing down from falling speed to zero, so the acceleration is the same. The big difference is in their size, or mass. And Newton's Law says that Force is made up of Mass times Acceleration (F=MA). So the bigger the mass in this experiment, the larger the force, and the bigger the crater!

TOP TIP!

If you use instant coffee, it's better if you can use powder and not granules.

WHAT HAPPENS IF...?

You can see and measure the various crater sizes caused by the different marbles. It's clear that the marble with the greatest mass created the largest crater. Now think about the shape and size of the marbles. Would a flat, wider object, such as a domino, create a larger crater than a marble of the same mass? Maybe you can see for yourself!

REAL-LIFE SCIENCE

The surface of the Moon is covered in craters caused by **meteors** crashing into it. Why isn't the Earth also covered in craters? There are some craters where huge meteors hit our planet, but most meteors burn up in our atmosphere—the friction of passing through the gases destroys them. The Moon has no atmosphere, so it has lots of craters.

Take a Pen for Spin

YOU WILL NEED

- Ballpoint pen
- DVD or CD
- Smooth floor or large table
- Sticky tack
- Ruler

How do you get a pen to stay upright without holding it? You can simply tuck it into a pencil holder—or you could use a bit of science to keep it balanced on nothing more than its own tip!

1

Hold the pen upright, so that its tip just touches the floor or table.

2

Spin it with a quick twist of your fingers, as if you were getting a spinning top started. The pen will fall over.

3

Wrap a piece of sticky tack (about twice the size of a pea) around the pen. It should be about 1 inch (3 cm) up from the tip.

4

Slide the DVD onto the pen and press it down firmly onto the sticky tack.

5

Now repeat steps 1 and 2, holding the pen upright and then spinning it like a top.

6

See how long the pen spins this time.

HOW DOES IT WORK?

You just demonstrated a scientific principle called angular **momentum**. Momentum describes the strength of a moving object. It's a combination of its mass and its **velocity**. A baseball bat has more momentum than a cardboard tube swung at the same speed because it has more mass. Angular momentum describes the strength of spinning objects. It also multiplies mass by velocity, and multiplies that by the **radius**. Adding the DVD and sticky tack to the pen added mass, and the width of the DVD lengthened the radius. The angular momentum increased, and the pen stayed upright!

TOP TIP!

Before you spin the pen the second time, hold it upright near the floor and make sure that the DVD is parallel to the floor. Adjust it if it's not.

WHAT HAPPENS IF...?

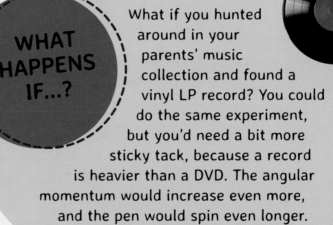

What if you hunted around in your parents' music collection and found a vinyl LP record? You could do the same experiment, but you'd need a bit more sticky tack, because a record is heavier than a DVD. The angular momentum would increase even more, and the pen would spin even longer.

REAL-LIFE SCIENCE

You've probably noticed angular momentum on bikes already, even if you didn't know the scientific term. Have you noticed that a bigger bicycle is steadier than a smaller one going the same speed? That's because the radius of the bigger bike's wheel is larger.

Hey—No Pressure!

Just how hard it is it to blow a couple of balloons away from each other? Pretty easy, you'd think...unless science stands in your way. You'll huff and you'll puff, but you'll wind up winded unless you read up on pressure!

YOU WILL NEED

- 2 balloons
- 2 high-backed chairs
- String
- Scissors
- Ruler
- Water from a tap
- Empty paper towel roll
- A broom

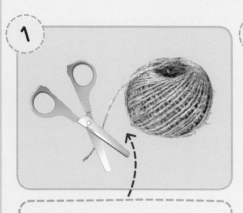

1
Cut two pieces of string, each about 20 inches (50 cm) long.

2
Run some cold water and slowly pour less than an inch (2.5 cm) into each balloon. Blow up the balloons and tie them.

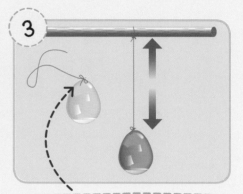

3
Tie a string to each balloon and tie the other end of each string loosely around the broom handle.

4
Arrange the chairs so that they're facing away from each other and rest the broom handle across the chair backs so that the balloons hang down.

5
Slide the balloons together, leaving 4 inches (10 cm) of space in between them. The water inside keeps them steady.

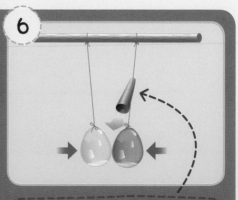

6
Crouch or kneel to the level to the balloons, hold the tube to your mouth, and blow hard between the balloons. Instead of moving away from each other, they're drawn together!

HOW DOES IT WORK?

You're supplying the force (your breath) to speed up a channel of air. And when air—or any other gas or liquid—begins to move faster, it loses pressure. Remember that air pressure is all around us, pushing in with a force of 14.7 pounds per square inch (1 kg per square cm). That force remains the same for all of the air surrounding the balloons, except for the fast-moving channel that you've created. That faster-moving air has less pressure, meaning it doesn't push so hard against the balloons. That's why they get pushed together.

REAL-LIFE SCIENCE

Engineers and architects need to understand the effects of varied air pressure on individual skyscrapers and groups of them. Sudden or extreme drops of pressure can put stress on those buildings, and it's important to have precautions built into them.

WHAT HAPPENS IF...?

Poke a hole through the bottom of a paper cup and stick a drinking straw through, plugging up any gaps with plasticine. Rest an inflated balloon on the cup and blow through the straw. As long as you're blowing, the balloon will remain attached to the cup, even if you tilt the cup down. It's that air pressure again.

the Balancing Forks

How good is your sense of balance?
This experiment uses a little bit of science
to pull off a trick that looks like magic.
The forks seem to be floating in mid-air,
but in fact they are just balanced—really well!

YOU WILL NEED

- 2 identical metal forks
- 2 toothpicks
- Sturdy salt shaker

1

Stick one of the toothpicks into a hole in the salt shaker so that it stands upright, like a flagpole. Hold the forks upright with their curved tines pointing at each other.

2

Push and "weave" the forks together so that their tines overlap. They should form an "x" shape, which you can balance on your finger beneath the crossed tines.

3

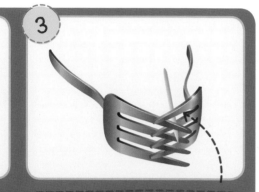

Feed the other toothpick through the first gap of the underside of the tines, then through the first gap of the other fork's tines.

4

You should be able to balance the arrangement on the end of your finger.

5

Carefully place the point of the second toothpick on the top point of the first toothpick. Remove your hand and the entire arrangement will balance on the two meeting points. It looks impossible!

HOW DOES IT WORK?

Of course, this wonderful display is not as impossible as it looks. It relies on the center of mass. Remember, this term refers to the "middle point" of an object, or collection of objects—so there's an equal amount of mass on either side.

Here, the center of mass is at the end of the toothpick that was stuck into the forks. Equal amounts of mass press in on it from all sides, keeping it secure. Even the force of gravity is "funneled" into this point, which is why people sometimes refer to the center of mass as the "center of gravity."

TOP TIPS!

It's easier to press the forks on a counter as you weave them together.

REAL-LIFE SCIENCE

Have you ever seen a tightrope walker make their way along a cable strung between two skyscrapers or across a deep canyon? A tightrope walker usually holds a long pole that juts out to either side of their body. The pole helps to keep the mass of the tightrope walker over the center of gravity—where their feet meet the cable—just as the long fork handles focus the center of gravity on the toothpick.

WHAT HAPPENS IF...?

Arrange about eight playing cards along the floor of a hallway, making a zigzag of "stepping stones" about 20 inches (50 cm) apart. Try walking along this path, only stepping on the cards. Now try it again while holding a broom handle for balance. Is it easier? Faster?

The Last Straw

YOU WILL NEED

- Glass jar with screw-on lid
- Plastic drinking straw
- Hammer
- Nail
- Poster putty
- Water or other drink

You've just had a long bike ride and you've come home thirsty. Look! Someone's made a cool drink for you, complete with a straw. Ahhh, just what you need. You take the straw in your mouth, begin to suck, and...nothing! What's going on?

1 Ask an adult to make a hole in the center of the lid using a hammer and nail.

2 See whether the straw fits through the hole. If not, ask the adult to widen the hole with the nail.

3 Feed the straw through the lid so that it will almost reach the bottom of the jar when the lid goes back on.

4 Put some poster putty around the straw where it meets the lid. This will make it airtight.

5 Fill the jar about ¾ full with a drink and screw the lid back on tightly. You can try to take a sip...

6 ...but you'll find that it's impossible!

26

HOW DOES IT WORK?

Sucking through a straw isn't so much about pulling (sucking) as it is about pushing. Air does the pushing, through the force known as air pressure. Normally, you suck in through the straw—which reduces the pressure inside your mouth. Meanwhile, the air all around the drink is pushing down on the top of the liquid in the glass. That pressure is greater than the reduced pressure in your mouth, so the drink gets pushed up the straw. But if you cover the drink completely, that outside air can't reach the liquid to push down on it... so you can't get any drink.

REAL-LIFE SCIENCE

You can see the effects of changing air pressure every day just by looking out the window. The Earth's spinning, teamed up with other factors such as the difference in temperature over land and over the ocean, affects air pressure. When areas of high pressure and low pressure meet, we get winds and other weather effects.

WHAT HAPPENS IF...?

You can try this trick the opposite way around. Stick a straw in the mouth of a half-full bottle of water and seal it with putty. Blow hard into the straw and then stand back. As soon as you stop blowing, water comes rushing out of the straw! Your blowing increased the pressure of the air inside the bottle so that it was greater than the air pressure outside.

Prepare for takeoff

How many times have you heard people say, "Well, it's not rocket science, is it?" This is a great experiment that really is about rocket science! Find a large space outside to conduct this experiment and get ready to say, "Mission accomplished!"

YOU WILL NEED

- 2 long, slim balloons
- Scissors
- Ruler
- 80 feet (25 m) of clear fishing line
- 2 pieces of drinking straw, each 1 inch (3 cm) long
- 1 empty 1-liter plastic bottle
- Masking tape
- A friend

1

Thread the two lengths of drinking straw on the fishing line.

2

80 feet (25 m)

Tie the fishing line between two strong objects, such as trees or tall fence posts. Make sure the line is taut.

3

1 inch (3 cm)

Cut a ring of plastic 1 inch (3 cm) wide from the middle of the plastic bottle.

4

Blow up one of the balloons and pinch it shut. Then press this pinched end into the plastic ring.

5

Press the pinched end of the first balloon against the ring while you insert the second balloon partway through the ring.

6

Now blow up the second balloon. Let go of the first balloon when it has been pressed firmly to the inside of the ring by the second balloon. Pinch the end of the second balloon.

7

Have your friend attach each balloon to a drinking straw (which are free to slide along the line). Pull the balloon combination to the end of the line.

8

Let go of the balloon and watch your rocket zoom along the line!

9

Partway down the line, the "first stage" (or second inflated balloon) should disconnect and fall behind.

Be careful when hanging up taut fishing line. People may not see it and hurt themselves.

HOW DOES IT WORK?

You seem to have mastered rocket science, but how exactly did you do it? It's all down to Newton's Third Law of Motion, which tells us that for every action there is an opposite and equal **reaction**. Letting go of the balloon means that the high-pressure air inside it rushes out of the back of the balloon. That motion, or "action," causes an opposite "reaction"—the force that sends the balloon forwards. The release of air from that first balloon also weakens its grip on the end of the second balloon, so the same action-reaction takes place a second time.

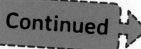

Continued

TOP TIPS!

When you walk the rocket back to one end of the line, make sure the pinched ends of the balloon are pointing backwards, so the rocket will go forwards!

This experiment works best if the fishing line is very taut and also level. This reduces friction along the track, letting the stages travel further.

WHAT HAPPENS IF...?

If you had enough friends helping you, do you think you could build a three-stage rocket? The missions to send astronauts to the Moon had three-stage rockets! How would you decide which balloons should be used for each stage?

REAL-LIFE SCIENCE

Since you've just built a rocket, you won't be surprised that space rockets work on the same basic principle as your model. Of course, they use special fuels such as liquid nitrogen instead of "balloon power," but they still rely on Newton's Laws of Motion. Your next stop—Mars?

Glossary

acceleration A change in speed.

center of mass The point that has the mass of an object evenly distributed around it, also called the center of gravity or balancing point.

ceramic Clay that has been baked and become hard.

crater A large bowl-shaped hole in the ground, made by an explosion or meteorite.

fluid A substance that has no fixed shape and can be moved by pressure.

force The strength of a particular energy at work.

gas A substance that can expand to fill any shape.

gravity The force that causes all objects to be attracted to each other.

inertia Staying unchanged until changed by an external force.

liquid A substance that flows freely but keeps the same volume.

mass A measure of how much matter something contains.

meteor A small rock or other substance that enters our atmosphere from outer space.

molecule The smallest unit of a substance, such as oxygen, that has all the properties of that substance.

momentum The amount an object moves.

predict To guess what will happen in the future as a result of an action.

pressure A physical force acting on or against an object by something in contact with it.

radius The distance from the center of a circle to the edge.

reaction Something that happens as a result of an action.

surface tension A force that binds molecules on the outer layer of a liquid together.

velocity The speed of something in a specific direction.

volume The amount of space a substance takes up inside a container.

Further Information

Books to read

Experiments with Forces by Anna Claybourne (Windmill Books, 2016)

Mind Webs: Forces and Motion by Anna Claybourne (Wayland, 2016)

Super Science: Feel the Force by Tom Adams and Thomas Flintham (Templar, 2011)

Websites

https://www.education.com/activity/forces/
Conduct fantastic experiments about forces at this fun site!

https://online.kidsdiscover.com/unit/force-and-motion
Check out this awesome site to learn more about forces.

http://www.dkfindout.com/us/science/forces-and-motion/
Explore this interactive site to learn about forces and motion!

Publisher's note to educators and parents: Our editors have carefully reviewed these websites to ensure that they are suitable for students. Many websites change frequently, however, and we cannot guarantee that a site's future contents will continue to meet our high standards of quality and educational value. Be advised that students should be closely supervised whenever they access the Internet.

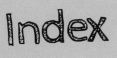
Index